# Born to be Wild

# Little Pigs

## Colette Barbé-Julien

Words that appear in the glossary are printed in
**boldface** type the first time they occur in the text.

GARETH**STEVENS**
GS
PUBLISHING
A Member of the WRC Media Family of Companies

# A Pen Full of Piglets

No baby pig ever comes into the world alone.  Often, ten or more little pigs are born at the same time.  Baby pigs are called piglets, and they are very active as soon as they are born.  They quickly run to their mother's belly to drink her milk.  Each piglet chooses and guards its own spot among her seven pairs of **teats**, or nipples.  If a piglet makes a mistake and picks a teat that one of its brothers or sisters has already claimed, it may be in for a fight.  When a mother pig has more than fourteen piglets in a **litter**, another female pig adopts the piglets the mother is not able to feed.

**At birth, a piglet weighs about 3 pounds (1.5 kilograms).  It has soft skin and tiny hairs called bristles.**

## What do you think ?

Why do farmers often separate a mother pig from her newborn piglets during the first couple of days?

a) She might crush them.

b) She does not love them yet.

c) The piglets are afraid of her.

3

A mother pig is often separated from her newborn piglets because she might crush them when she lies down.

A mother pig is called a sow. She carries her babies in her body for 114 days — three months, three weeks, and three days. When she is almost ready to give birth, she makes a nest of straw and lies down. The pig farmer helps the sow give birth and places the piglets under a heat lamp so they stay warm. A newborn piglet is **delicate**. It needs heat, quiet, and a clean place without cold drafts or wet ground. Every two hours, the farmer takes the little pigs to their mother so they can drink her milk. Keeping the piglets away from their mother the rest of the time prevents her from crushing her babies when she lies down or rolls over.

Piglets are born with their eyes open, but they will never see very well. Pigs do, however, have excellent hearing.

4

A sow protects her piglets. If an unfamiliar animal or human comes near, she may become angry and mean.

A male pig is called a boar. If a boar has had an operation so it cannot be a father, then it is called a barrow. "Hog" is a word that is used to mean any kind of pig.

Pigs have four toes on each foot, but they walk on only the two front toes. Their two back toes do not even reach the ground.

# A Hungry Little Pig

A newborn piglet has a very big appetite.  It drinks milk from its mother several times a day.  A sow produces lots of milk — up to 3 gallons (11 liters) every day.  Her milk is twice as rich as cow's milk.  Drinking only its mother's milk, a piglet doubles its birth weight in just ten days. A piglet drinks milk for about one month, then it begins to eat other kinds of food.  Farmers feed pigs all the food they need to grow and stay healthy, but pigs also like to dig around in the dirt to find roots, leaves, insects, and earthworms to eat.

## What do you think?

About how much does a piglet weigh when it is two months old?

a) 22 pounds (10 kg)

b) 33 pounds (15 kg)

c) 44 pounds (20 kg)

A pig has a very strong sense of smell.  Its flat nose is called a snout.  Piglets quickly learn to use their snouts to furrow, or dig, in the dirt to find food.

When it is two months old, a piglet weighs about 44 pounds (20 kg).

On pig farms, a piglet may be **weaned** and separated from its mother when it is one month old. But the young pig will continue to grow! Pigs gain a lot of weight, and they grow a thick layer of fat under their skin. Because pigs are raised for their meat, people let them eat as much food as they want. By the time a pig is six months old, it will weigh about 220 pounds (100 kg).

**Instead of waiting for feeding time with its brothers and sisters, this hungry piglet is sneaking in an extra meal!**

In every litter, some piglets are bigger and stronger than others. The smallest piglet is often the first one born.

A sow lies down to feed her babies, so the piglets have no trouble finding their spots. The piglets that feed the closest to their mother's head will put on weight faster because her front teats produce more milk.

# What Pigs Like to Do

At first, all newborn piglets do is drink milk and sleep. Very soon, however, they begin to play in their pens. Brother and sister piglets push and shove each other, roll around in the straw, and climb all over their mother when she lies down. When the piglets are about three weeks old, they are strong enough to leave the pen, and they run all over the place, squealing with delight. Their mother grunts to calm them down and to let them know they are safe. She watches over her babies and keeps them from straying too far from her.

Pigs that know each other will greet one another by touching their snouts together. By their movements and grunts, pigs show when they are happy, afraid, or angry.

## What do you think?

Why do little pigs like to roll around in the mud?

a) They like being dirty.

b) They want to cool off and kill the insects on their bodies.

c) They like to make their mothers angry.

**Little pigs roll around in the mud to cool off and kill the insects on their bodies.**

Pigs do not sweat so, when the weather is hot, they cool off by taking mud baths. Lying in mud also gets rid of insects and keeps a pig's skin soft. But pigs like to be clean, too! Each pig has its own place to go to the bathroom and another place where it sleeps. In a group of pigs that lives outside, the strongest pigs will get the most comfortable spots to sleep. Pigs have peaceful lives divided between looking for food and napping.

When the weather is cold, little pigs stay warm in their pens by snuggling together in the straw.

When a sow drinks water, she makes the ground around her wet and muddy. Then all the pigs roll in the mud. The mud keeps the pigs cool and protects their skin from sunburn.

Pigs are quick and can run fast. After they have grown fatter, however, and their **lungs** are squeezed between huge amounts of flesh, they are not able to run fast for very long distances or for long periods of time.

Kept warm by their layers of fat, adult pigs are not afraid of snow. They even eat it sometimes. Snow is a great source of water.

# Pigs Eat Everything!

A pig farmer provides the food that pigs need to gain weight, but a little pig also learns to use its snout to find food. By sniffing and digging with its snout, a pig finds worms, snails, insects, lizards, and even mice to eat! Pigs **graze** on wild plants, such as dandelions and grass, as well as on plants grown just for them, such as alfalfa and clover. Pigs that have a chance to explore a forest will eat any hazelnuts, acorns, chestnuts, and mushrooms they find there.

## What do you think?

Since a pig eats both plants and meat, what is it called?

a) an eat-everything

b) an omnivore

c) an allivore

Long ago, some pigs ate only foods they found in the wild, such as acorns that had fallen to the ground. Today, in **Corsica**, you can still see pigs roaming freely in groves of chestnut trees looking for nuts.

**Because a pig eats both plants and meat, it is called an omnivore.**

For hundreds of years, most pigs living on farms ate kitchen leftovers, including vegetable peelings, bread, and meat scraps. Farmers also mixed in whatever crops they grew in their fields. Today, a pig's menu has more variety and includes cereals, all kinds of fruits, and vegetables such as cooked potatoes, carrots, cabbages, and beets. Pigs also eat milk products and food made from soybeans.

**Because pigs have an excellent sense of smell, they are raised, in some places, to search for truffles. Pigs love to eat truffles, too, so when a pig finds a truffle, the farmer must be ready to stop the pig from gobbling it up.**

**Truffles are mushrooms that grow underground, usually near tree roots. Many people like to use truffles in cooking, but because they are hard to find, they are also very expensive.**

A female pig needs to drink up to 11 gallons (40 l) of water a day when she is feeding her piglets milk. Some farmers add water to a sow's food to make sure she is getting enough.

Like all animals that eat plants, pigs have pointed **incisors** at the front of their mouths, but like animals that eat meat, they also have well-developed **canine teeth**. A piglet has thirty-two baby teeth. An adult pig has a total of forty-four teeth, including twelve incisors and four canine teeth.

Sticking its snout in a trough of good food must be fun, because a pig always gobbles up everything it finds there.

# Pig Pals

In picture books, pigs are almost always pink and have curly tails, but not all pigs look like that. Pigs can be white or black — or white and black! They can also be reddish or gray. Some pigs have only a little hair, while other pigs are almost as hairy as some dogs. Their ears might stand straight up, or stick straight out, or hang downward. Pigs do not all weigh the same amount, and they often look very different from each other, too. Some of the older **breeds**, or kinds, of pigs are not as fat as some of the newer breeds.

**This young pig has a pink and black body and ears that stick straight out. When it is fully grown, it will be about 4 feet (1.2 meters) long and weigh 350 pounds (159 kg).**

## What do you think?

How much do full grown male pigs weigh?

a) up to 660 pounds (300 kg)

b) up to 880 pounds (400 kg)

c) up to 1,100 pounds (500 kg)

**Full grown male pigs can weigh up to 1,100 pounds (500 kg).**

The newest breeds of pigs were developed to create the heaviest possible animals. Two-hundred years ago, people in England were the first to improve pig breeds. They crossed large English pigs with Asian pigs, which were small but had litters with many babies. Asia has many different kinds of pigs, and Asian pigs often wander loose in villages. In some parts of the world, pigs live in people's homes and are as much a pet as a family dog!

The name for this pig breed is Large White. The males grow to 6 feet (2 m) long and weigh 1,100 pounds (500 kg). The Large White breed was started by mixing English and Asian pigs. Today, they are the most common pigs in Europe.

Adult Corsican pigs do not weigh more than 285 pounds (130 kg). With their dark color and thick fur, they look like wild boars.

Chinese pigs are small and black, with wrinkled skin. They are quiet and obedient animals, and the females have many litters of piglets.

A Vietnamese potbelly pig has dark skin, very short feet, and a wrinkled snout. The ears of this **dwarf** breed are small and straight.

Pigs are **mammals**. They can be found on every continent except Antarctica. Until about eight or nine thousand years ago, pigs were wild. They were first brought to the Americas in 1493 by Christopher Columbus, on his second voyage. Today, there are about ninety different breeds of pigs. Eight breeds are raised in the United States. Pigs live between twelve and twenty-seven years.

Domestic pigs are related to some wild animals that have hooves, including wild boars; warthogs; African river hogs; **peccaries**, which are also called javelinas; and even hippopotamuses.

Most piglets are born with curly tails. To keep little pigs from biting each others tails, farmers often cut off the tails.

A pig's skin is covered with straight hairs called bristles. People use pigs' hair to make brushes.

Because it has such a short neck, a pig cannot turn its head very far to either side.

Pigs have large ears and an excellent sense of hearing.

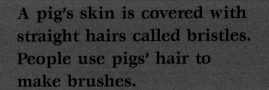

A pig's eyes are small, and its vision is not very good.

The snout of a pig is shaped like a disk. It is made of muscles and bony tissue.

Pigs have four toes on each foot. Their thick toenails form hooves. The two toes at the back of each foot do not touch the ground.

# GLOSSARY

**breeds** — (n) groups of animals, with the members in each group having the same basic features, behaviors, and abilities

**canine teeth** — sharp, pointed teeth on both sides of the mouth

**Corsica** — an island in the Mediterranean Sea that is part of France

**delicate** — easily hurt or broken

**dwarf** — describes a living thing that is much smaller than normal size

**graze** — to feed on grass and other growing plants

**incisors** — front teeth that are used for cutting

**litter** — a group of young animals born at the same time to the same mother

**lungs** — the parts of the body used for breathing

**mammals** — warm-blooded animals that have backbones, give birth to live babies, feed their young with milk from the mother's body, and have skin that is covered with hair or fur

**peccaries** — wild, piglike animals that live in South America and the southwestern United States

**teats** — the nipplelike body parts on a female animal's belly, through which milk is drawn

**truffles** — mushrooms that grow under the ground

**weaned** — used to eating solid foods instead of only drinking mother's milk

Please visit our web site at: **www.garethstevens.com**
For a free color catalog describing Gareth Stevens Publishing's list of high-quality books and multimedia programs, call 1-800-542-2595 (USA) or 1-800-387-3178 (Canada). Gareth Stevens Publishing's fax: (414) 332-3567.

Library of Congress Cataloging-in-Publication Data

Barbé-Julien, Colette.
[Petit cochon. English]
Little pigs / Colette Barbé-Julien. — North American ed.
p. cm. — (Born to be wild)
ISBN-10: 0-8368-6698-3 — ISBN-13: 978-0-8368-6698-8 (lib. bdg.)
1. Piglets—Juvenile literature. I. Title. II. Series.
SF395.5B3713 2007
636.4'07—dc22
2005037418

This North American edition first published in 2007 by
**Gareth Stevens Publishing**
A Member of the WRC Media Family of Companies
330 West Olive Street, Suite 100
Milwaukee, Wisconsin 53212 USA

This U.S. edition copyright © 2007 by Gareth Stevens, Inc.
Original edition copyright © 2004 by Mango Jeunesse.

First published in 2004 as *Le petit cochon* by Mango Jeunesse, an imprint of Editions Mango, Paris, France. Additional end matter copyright © 2007 by Gareth Stevens, Inc.

Picture Credits (t=top, b=bottom, l=left, r=right)
Bios: C. Ruoso title page, 4, back cover; Klein/Hubert 2; J. F. Mutzig 10; F. and J. L. Ziegler 12(t); J. J. Alcalay 15; Bergerot/Robert 20; M. Gunther 21(b); D. Halleux 22. Cogis: D. and S. Simon front cover, 7, 8, 17(b); Lanceau 5(l), 5(b), 12(b), 17(t); Gehlhar 16(l). Colibri: F. and J. L. Ziegler 5(t), 9(both), 17(r), 22–23; G. Abadie 13(t); Ch. Testu 21(t); A. M. Loubsens 21(l). Sunset: H. Reinhard 13(b); G. Lacz 16(r), 18.

English translation: Deirdre Halat
Gareth Stevens editor: Barbara Kiely Miller
Gareth Stevens art direction: Tammy West
Gareth Stevens designer: Kami Strunsee

Printed in the United States of America
1 2 3 4 5 6 7 8 9 10 09 08 07 06